THE MEMORY OF THE DUSTWHISTLER

I0162659

and other poems

nishíth singh

2014

Copyright © 2014 nishíth singh
All rights reserved.
ISBN-13: 978-0615953045
ISBN-10: 0615953042

DEDICATION

To the burning.
To the relinquished.

Acknowledgments..i

1   Rome Leaves Us Every Time We Visit History.............................1
2   To Live Once More..2
3   Just Because There Is So Much Time.............................4
4   A Personal Object Called Face...5
5   The Memory Of A Rose...6
6   The Mirror Traveler...7
7   Scorpions...8
8   Why Should I Fear Those Frontier-less Eyes.....................9
9   The Labyrinthweavers...10
10   Sparrow-cluttered Homes..12
11   The Page Of Rose..14
12   There Have Been Days...15
13   The Story Wrong...16
14   The Book In Your Hand...17
15   On The Solitude Of Mothers And Stars............................18
16   The Destiny Of Faces..19
17   On So Many Occasions..20
18   Montage Of Our Personal Journeys..................................22
19   The Great Picker..24
20   Images Of Symmetry...25
21   The Memory Of The Dustwhistler.....................................26
22   Life Speaks To Desire..27
23   The Train That Leaves My Home......................................28
24   I Want To Forget You In The Urging Dusk........................29
25   A Petition To The Past...30
26   We Are Lovers..31
27   The Omitted Color Of Things...32
28   The End Of The Poem...33
29   Our Pawned Hearts...34
30   Long Before The Kiss..35
31   Once Upon A Time...36

32	Light	37
33	Martha's Wait	38
34	The Tectonic Dream	40
35	A Plea For The Choice Of Silence	41
36	Solitude Of A Christmas	42
37	Clouds From A Giant's Bread	44
38	She Is El Salvador	46
39	The Lives Of Others	47
40	Between The Columns Of Hours	48
41	When We Were Young	49
42	All Chance Is Woman	50
43	American Serenade	52
44	What Matters Is The Glow	53
45	Why Not Merely Her	54
46	Woman Is Any Dusk	55
47	My Hour And My Scripture	56
48	Bird	57
49	An Appeal For Correctness	58
50	Journey	59
51	In The Silence Of A Mortal's Bedroom	60
52	The Day After The Oklahoma Tornado	62
53	A Pact With Solitude	64

ACKNOWLEDGMENTS

Grateful, to Camille Carter and Bonnie Braendlin and Hans Braendlin
for their step-by-step guidance, love and
unconditional support; to Souvik Maitra for the cover photograph; to
everyone whom I have ever known, to their hands that have nudged me
safe into this future where poetry was permitted in my living, bound as
we pass through the impossible labyrinths of happenings, of memories.

Rome Leaves Us Every Time We Visit History

All stars are past
The planets, the sun is past
Their light left them years ago
We are past of today
With you the unbroken light left us years ago

All destruction is teamwork
The pursuit of perfection is the beginning of monstrosity
The loss of Rome, the end of Rome
Crumbled and brittle like an old page
Is the beginning of this arrogant world
Like Rome, you leave each time we visit our memories
Our elected promises, our more than one afternoon
You are the beginning of all that is no longer beautiful
No longer the gentle sun, the delicate blood
Goodbye now the pavement of dreams
Goodbye now the verse of yours
That sat on the lips like practiced God

You are alone
As the unending moon
As the alphabet that seeks the historian's pen
And I am lost and sweating
In a crowd of your absences

In my honoring solitude you have been unknown to me
Perhaps I feel happy to have not met you
Happy to have only understood you in your great absences
After all, a meeting is the beginning of illusions
A meeting is the origin of otherness

You breathe in my hours
Hiding and awake like a cat coiled in the dark
A stray perfume in the funeral crowd
Your absence consigns me to an ancient festival of melancholy
Its secret way of showing
That it is in you we proceed to be
Your fading away in the thoughts of arrested noons
Is my going from myself
The world is separation
Slow are the continents that drift
Quick the soldier departs in the appetite of wars

But do not be unseen any more
Longer than the small string of years we have been granted
Come when the evening exhales our wearied spirits
And our thoughts rejoice
To see those leaves roll along the asphalt
Come to me
Where the sight of a fast mad world graffities you on my heart
Where your name is a mural carved on the solid vapors of sighs
When every sleep is a visit to an unreachable compendium of kisses
Come to me then
Bring my abandoned me with you
I want to live once more

Just Because There Is So Much Time

Just because there is so much time
Between the secret histories of births
And the mystery of our ends
Shouldn't we be doing something
Like, attending a school
Waking up to the nonsense of manipulated hours
Tasting alcohol amid the giggle and the smoke wheels of dorms
Let us find someone to live with
In the transparence of days, in the opacity of nights
Shall we fetch her flowers on her bad days
To make her happy once again

Since there is so much time
Let me call mother
Ask if she took her blue pill today
Ask her again if father is well
Let us watch our child toe about the resonant rooms
Let us watch the child attend college
And become an office worker
So that he can afford a phone
For the purpose of finding the best nursing home for us both
Where they will bring us blankets within an hour of the behest
And wipe from our toes the urine dripping like comets
All for a nominal charge
So let us go do something
Like relentless groceries, bloodbaths of discounts
Since there still is so much of that amethyst color time
To kill
Between the moment of our birth
And
The patient hour of the grave

A Personal Object Called Face

On a putty of flesh
Time carves a thing
Puts a nose in between
Two eyes go bling

Dolled up in hair trim
I launder it, I have it starched
Felt the saddest in years
When the cruel pimples marched

Wrinkles on their way
My mirror dares say
Like a shirt iron-pressed
Can the doctor make it stretch

I carry it to church
I bring it to the store
Washed squeaky at night
It sings me a snore

I can spare you my house
Have that soul of mine replaced
Sorry, it's not for the taking
It's my face, it's my face

The Memory Of A Rose

A rose never forgets
The date
The divorce
The rose breeds memories on the table
The rose has angles and point of views in the vase
A rose is a physical symptom
Of calculus and progressions
In some poems
Rose unravels time
Rose weaves months

A rose dies unspoken
A rose does not indulge
In beginnings and ends
A rose remains unknown among so many known roses
A rose thinks to hide under the dew
A rose startles with its thorns
A rose is in the rest
A rose is in reproach
A rose is origin, a rose is original
A rose travels in hands and pockets
A rose on the pulpit
A rose in the pit
A rose a clot under the soldier's boot
A rose half whirled
Is a poem abandoned
A rose to be
A rose not to be

The Mirror Traveler

Who does my mirror home
Perhaps a traveler
He flashes quickly between its scintillating edges
And in all these years of hide and seek
Gets the lines of old age tattooed
That the steel-tipped timeneedles make on his face

He shows up over and over, reliably so in all mirrors
Only to fade one day along with his companion
I, his companion, who is locked outside of the mirrors
Peering down the mirror from my world
A world of restaurants, Amazons, chandelier rooms
A world of gods, epithets
And George W. Bush
I peer from my ruins that are my cities and sometimes, Venice
Looking into the eternal alleys of reflections
And for that lost moment
On the verge of a sea of tears
Longing to say, I miss you. I always have. I always have.

Standing before the flat waterwoven silver
My hands comb a bizarre landscape of scalps
I whisper a prayer, everyday
Into the ears of my gloomy image, that traveler inside
The one who prides in imitating me
Who never adjourns that reunion of faces, the show of knuckles
Who grimaces after me
And who is wondering too
How did we get into this game of prisons that are our worlds
Where do we all go from here

In our villages
Beneath the innocent stones and boulders
Under their moist underbellies where the scented earth is
We used to turn and uncover, without a warning
So many startled scorpions, hiding for eternities
Cast in a watery gold
Whom the frigid sunlight has never touched
Their own surprise stings them now
Angry and curled would be the scorpions, revolting and asking
Who turned our stones, our homes, our perceptions

Raging, skeptics of an open cosmos
An insulted humanity we are like the scorpions
Our bright dawns uncovers and wakes us up
Stung by nostalgia we step out and stare into the heavens
Protesting and questioning, our whys and our whats
Our many heads like a basket of eggs
A confused great crowd we live
Under the vast white bellies of our cloudboulders

Why Should I Fear Those Frontier-less Eyes

Why should I fear those frontier-less eyes
And the dismissals they insist
Have they not promised me the best privileges of solitude
That the schools, ticket lines, camps, campuses, lectures
Had once robbed our youth of
Only to return the loneness in its far unrewarding, lifeless versions
Like bank balances, endings of vacations, living rooms, waiting rooms

The Labyrinthweavers

They live in our rooms
Under our comforters
Caught in the crackling planes of days and nights
Capturing autumns in photo-flash machines
Stretched between the sleeping and the awake time
You and I, the Labyrinthweavers
They are weaving desires, they are yarning stories
Day after day, night after night

One day they saw them strewn on the battlegrounds
The other day
They were seen plowing the emerald fields for food
Protesting in carnivals
Feeding their babies in their ochre slums
Rich in cars and rich in pains
Confusion of heroes, victims of fame
You and I, the Labyrinthweavers
They are weaving reminiscences, they knit the states of mind

They are on our palms
That ungraspable tribe whose voice rings in our ears
Inventors of God and cocaine
Whose greatest pain is the awareness of Paradise
Always a better world out there they tell each other of
While they are burning up the forests that once was their home
Chasing after the last teasings of immortality
Every tusk, every horn, every impossible insect is their aphrodisiac
Wrapped up in woven textiles of fantasies
Radios bring them forth
And crucified by democracies
They ride in buses and smile in advertisements
Standing in a ritual called line
Uncottoning dreams in remote beds
They cry when the loved ones leave
They are ragdolls in hospitals
Watered and needled in their own voodoos
Televisions reveal their stained teeth
Newspapers talk of their bad and good deeds
They are they and we, you and I
The Labyrinthweavers
And when they will be done scheming their occult travesties
And this eternal din collapses
We will say of their work
See what we have done my friend

Sparrow-cluttered Homes

Those who are not destined to die
And, hence, never meant to be born
Will they not miss the vanity, the merry nonsense of taking birth
And the fun in slithering about in operating rooms
Naked, feather-plucked, like a seal

Those who will not see the ten o' clock of mankind's nights
How will they ever cinder in the afternoons lost on them

Those who never fell, head on asphalt, knees on nails
Shall never know the taste of waiting in lines for tinctures

The ones who denounce mirrors
Will they ever discover the impossible equations in wrinkles
And the silent sculpture of time, trust and cheap soaps
That is their face

Those who never commit a single spelling mistake
Or have forgotten their keys and glasses
Only to recall them while standing in tint-glassed church halls
Or have never spat across a table of dignified, dyspeptic guests
They miss the stupidity that embraces us without prejudice

Those who never dare to solve the final structures of dreams
Those who refuse to recognize aftermaths and longevity
The renegade tramps, the wanderers, the free spirits
Will they not miss tragedies, computers, constipations, religions
Salaries, toasters, marriages, commercials

Those who think they have heard the truth
Are they not lying to their dementias

And the sorry lovers who think
They will never see her again waiting by the sill
With a vow around her wrist, pink dress, and eyes traced by sorrows
Are they not betraying their superstitions

Will they ever feel how
With each breath
And with every false sentence they beget
They become another, same as others

There are even those
Who believe the past is forever gone
But every time their fingers kiss an old photograph
And every time they hear their frail mother's voice invented by phones
With each act of reaching out to that latent corridor
They set off vertiginous futures
And find themselves imprisoned
In an impenetrable forest
Erected by nostalgia
That feels as real, as secret, as warm
As once home did
The invisible, blood-red, sparrow-cluttered home

They saw the coming of the night
Their world drowning in the dark
Their world all slight
They said it was over
It is written all over

Not one among them saw the hope
In our morning's prose
The darkness scribed with dew
On the page of rose

There Have Been Days

There have been days
All my days in fact
When I have toiled lucklessly
To capture the dazzle brimming her face
In this false and bitter architecture of words
Looking for it everywhere
In the swirls on a coffee by the busy street of hawkers
In the outcry of forests, in the lash of the sea

There have been moments
In fact all my moments that there have been
I have spent soliciting
The covert warfare of her gaze through time
Dying with a hope to bottle it

There are futures
In fact all of the futures
Lie in the siege of her hair cast
These are the same futures I am bound to waste
Looking for the meaning of equations
In the intersecting petals and in the unspoken words

And there are such pasts
All of my pasts in fact
Where I was to discover
Only this late in time's yarn
Right on my deathbed
That I have been spending the years bygone
Without my knowing
In search for that elusive museum of emptiness
She had walked into once in an October hail

He who swears by his deeds
By his work, by his creed
Proclaims that mortality of man is final, death is pure
And yet his soul knows not
For there are more things
Purer than his vanity, holier than his wisdom
Far purer are the moods of moon that drowns in the cloud
The gleam of a dying leaf in rain
Far purer are the rumor of the flowers
The color of their hearth
And the murmur of their birth
Waiting sweet and dead
In her hair's warm earth

This world accepts the book in your hand
There are more books
Indivisible books, consumed by molds
The ones unknowable to the clans of printing machines
And the one whose shreds are strewn
In a war awakened rubble somewhere in Russia
Books that I, the styled up ignorant, shall never see
Perhaps the hour of our next pain
And the name of the next victim
Is indexed in its premonitory pages
Or written in primitive calligraphy
Across its curved, historical spine
That book shall go forever unread
One slice of cosmos thrives veiled to our eyes
No wonder papá keeps saying
The future is an unknown street
Where minutes will drag us by our ears
Where there is no memory
And from where comes no voice

On The Solitude Of Mothers And Stars

When I was little, you pointed the heaven's stars to me
I wish then, mother mine, I had known your sacrifices
The solitude you would wake up to bear
In the fire of afternoons, in the nightnag of ices

With all the worldly means I possess
Let alone your years lost and sintered out in the sun
I wish I could buy back one second of yours
Your one youth's smile, your one sigh gradual as the Nile
Your cherished moment
In which you had felt the kicks of my feet selfish
With all the hubris of education I carry
With all the vain certificates
I wish I could wipe the sweat that beads your brow
Peel off the skin of wrinkles in which you live you grow
And that makes you look an old lake mother mine
Caressed by the sweeping breath of time

When I was small, you pointed the stars to me
Today, in the remembered inspiration of our stars
Mother mine can I give you a poem today
For that warm in your soul indelible and loving
Each word of the poem
Shall be an echo of your lullabies so living so forgiving
Your son, my mother in a world so apart
Brings you a poem buried in my heart
A poem that is a memorial for your untold scars
A poem raised in the solitude of our shared night stars

If there be a face foreordained
For a newspaper's front page
One to reflect London's sunshine
One for the eyes of the velvet monarch
And one for mother mine
Whose face switched with yours in the yearbook
Whose shall the next Jew's nose choose
Whose face squished will you be born with
And whose shall the crumbling Rushmore lose

If there be
A face old in the memory of the alchemist
One in Peru wetted by the Amazon rain
One for Oklahoma's dust to plaster and kiss
And one staring lost from a slow iron train
Whose face did your mirror show you today
Whose did the postcard from Istanbul contain
Whose face shall I bring to your deserted door
Whose face shall reveal your unquenchable pain

Food must have its misdeeds
For which the teeth have been punishing it for ages

A doctor does not quite cure
He merely exists between the coming and the leaving

A pastor is not an access to Providence
He is the one walking hurriedly
From one confession to the next
Just so that he does not miss the exciting bits

An archway might be a historical structure
It is also the devil's tongue cleaner

There are no cars
There are steel lice of the landscape

Man is not merely a mammal in ugly shorts
He is everyone who ever came from the office irritated
A perpetual soldier at war on growing beards, nails, being late

A woman is not that neighbor
She is a good-looking existential typhoon

A father does not die
He discovers the perfect way to get rid of that loud woman on the sofa
After forty two wishful years

Old age is not only the end of youth
It is a long inaugural ceremony of televisions and irritability
It is an orchestra of the creaking joints

A family is not that noisy throng that lives among furniture
It is a quick gathering of life travelers on their way to their funerals

Birthdays are not a cult for those who have lived that far
They are days on which pretty cakes will be slaughtered

Darkness cannot merely be the subtraction of bulbs
Darkness is the radiant evening that I refused to perceive
Even as she kept pointing to it
On so many occasions

Montage Of Our Personal Journeys

We have come far
So far our legs have grown weary
We have seen our cousins born and bred
And loved ones in shreds
From afar we hear them
Our kin, our glowing people
Their hands chiseling the various geographies of mud
Ireland and India, the singsong jungles in Africa
My race swallows me and spits me in many directions
It is the need of man to move to fascinating prairies
We set off to the beckoning other
Newer earths that seek us in return

We took a decision once
To interrupt the ties of salt and womb
In desire of continents distant
In desire of the beautiful sun coloring their horizons
We broke up with the warmth of once photographed dawns
We have shed the skin
Our mothers had once oiled
Our feelings have to travel in reminiscences
Saltier and thicker than the sweat of childhood summers

We have come so far
Our souls beg for the drop
Of that rain our young eyes beheld once
Washing dust from the leaves and from the countenances of grandparents
From our lands, our epochs, we are distant
The blood of our roots is alive in our veins
The eyes of our brothers
Tile the walls in memories
Yet so far that from this spot and these senile eyes
The house and the porch we grew up in
Everything is amour, every light is sugary vintage

We have come this far
Our legs feel weary and ancient
Our hearts are sinking in nostalgia's quicksand
They still beat for what was once ours
The clay horse and the exalting echoes of mothers
The streets we played have grown brittle in dreams
We have crossed many sadness, many oceans
To touch and feel new cities, new homes, sweeter solitudes
Our toes cliff a future now
In our journeys we have met our lovers
Those souls deep as twilights
This far from our birthlands we take another step
A sojourn in sunshine
A protest against inertia
Move we must
For in movement is parting, parting reveals love
And we hope time scissors on the cloth of our wanting spirit
All that is cherished
All that was abandoned

The Great Picker

You know since you left
I have much grown
No longer the lounger great
No more the poet lone

I have made myself a name
In the abandonment of yours
Now they call me the Great Picker
They find me always on all fours

If you happen to pass before the parlor
You will see me gathering the many shreds of my life
Confetti of butterflies, shreds of our noon
Upon which my fate ran its knife

The parrot darn ate a few
A few my forgetfulness takes
The breeze that caresses your empty chair
Sweeps few away in its unfeeling wake

And yet quite a bit I have saved
Working day and working night
I know there remain a few in your clutch
But I am not here for a fight
You can keep our moments best
And all the rest
All I ask you, so sea-blue, so gracious
Put an end to this heartless test

Nature embodies symmetry
My modern song has an ancestor
In the heartbeats of an unknown primeval tribe
Every act, every motion has its secret twin
The distant hills tango with the eyes in the windows of a passing train
Sun tangoes shadows on the surface of earth

I am destined to place words on the page
Like a mason puts bricks on his imaginary wall
The velocity of a blue bird on Monday is the same
As the hotness of a black man's blood who once rose in the shackles
In that mirror of old time I was a Jew
The one who dies third in row in the photograph

The windings of this world go around a mysterious equipoise
With movements and webs
The spider courts the secret graph of God in my yard

The Memory Of The Dustwhistler

In a time of good year, my mother you were near
Funny anecdotes you would tell in the noon's infernal spell
We braved the winter's chisel with your song, with your whistle
When your bosom went dry you brought sugarcane to try
We were busy hunting our tomorrows in the rich man's eye

It was a good time of year, my mother you were near
Today, in a cinema of memory I watch you mother
Your bangle of ivory, your face of leather
In the streets we would trust, we were the gypsies in dust
Now long you are gone in the bequeathing rain of life
In that rain we saw you wilt, in that rain we all rust

In this life
I have asked for twilight
And for one good night
Demanding life's forgiving fire
With a heart reverberating in desires

And they kept coming to me
With a tinted day, with its blood-filled twilight
Crimson, warm and glowing bright
Until came the daggers of time
Slaughtered that twilight mine
And then right before my reverent eyes
At the end of my dying twilight
Raised in its blood, black with might
I saw standing my shining night
For these are the secret judgments of life
For every twilight gone
For every twilight no longer mine
There arrives a night infinite
There comes a night fine

The Train That Leaves My Home

What good is the sunshine
Even if it were to do the favor
And announce my face to the mirrors today
The same face an old mother thinks of everyday
Sitting pretty and motionless at her porch
Watching those who pass before that house of mine

What is the purpose of the tears
Even those that bear the strength
To bring back that love of mine
When the clouds have vowed
To waste the tears on my village
When I am no longer there running on the red gravel

What shall I do with these poems
She once refused to read
If grows the quiet night
And my distant family shuts all the windows
Not aware of their lost son
Reading aloud a thousand miles away
Hoping that the final stanza might be the one
In which her best forms have been revealed

Who needs sadness anymore
The one I felt yesterday
In her voice over the phone
That sadness is the only chord, my only accomplice
My guitar shall know to play it tomorrow
When I am aboard the ruthless train
That leaves my home

I Want To Forget You In The Urging Dusk

I shall forget you in the urging dusk
At any given instant, at any mortal moment
Only if it was known to me
Which one of the memories is you
Were you the steel colored afternoon
In which I had waited for the ice cream vendors
So that I could buy one for you with my pocket change
And bring it to you where you always stood in a frock
Underneath the enduring blue dome that is the sky

I shall stop dreaming of you
But I don't know which one of the images is you
Are you the shadows in the neon garden
The hairdresser in New Orleans
Or the naquaabed princess solitary in the mausoleum
Where distances and tears pave your earth
Were you the empress lost to your Revlon sadness
In that billboard there
Were you the one standing under the street light in Tokyo
Whom the adolescence of rapid cities sidetracks

My memory would have forsaken you long ago
Had I known how you looked
On that evening when violins were painting your church
And I was there right before you
Holding your hand that dreams of touching flowers
And you had smiled an arc
Slicing through the sunset needling your eyes
It was a smile in whose flicker live my lamps, my burning noon

A poem for those who recall and count their remote afternoons on their fingers, but don't write them down anywhere.

A Petition To The Past

Be kind my past
Return my best hours that I had lived once
Without a single sparkle of her remembrance
Without any of these longings of today
The ones I am left with now
The poems I am capable of beckoning now
Only favor the deserts and the autumns
Only belch dust and powdery crickets

My past must you refuse me
The coronation of my former nights
The cushion of that quietude lost
Bereft I shall proceed to ask my living present
For the poems and the minutes that pass before me now
Without sense or stillness
And I shall beg my tomorrows
To bring me that unanimous hour of death
Where the memory and the loss are final

Waiting on the doors of their breaths we are the unheard knocks
We are leaves in the breeze of a sigh's abiding hope
We are keepsakes of your reminiscences
We are lovers
Of the evenings glittering with your smiles that are like the bridge lights
We stand in embrace before the high walls of fortifications
On the asphalt roads where sad gypsies stroll
Under the windows in Lisbon where lamps and old ladies wait
In the helpless New Orleans ruins eaten by water
Among the doves echoing in an emperor's tomb
We are born in the ripples of a world surplus in quartz tears
We shall earn our final melancholy
In the quiet uproar of your heartbeat
An we shall fade in the exhales of your perspirations

The Omitted Color Of Things

When I see a fort
I see the strength in its stones
And its dust upholstery
I don't see the hands of time headstrong, chipping at the edges
Nor the infinite will of flowers pushing through the cracks

When I see a parent
I see diabetes and marble brittle joints
I don't see the moment of his child's birth
Still living strong in him
That makes him be

When I see her
I see the sheen of a capitalistic shampoo
The poverty of flowers
Not the uplifting strength of maternity
Universe and mother they are the same

When I see my face in the mirror
I see the wrinkles
And the escaping hours of life
I don't see the granted freedom
To dream the color of things imminent
To rejoice the color of scenes bygone

The End Of The Poem

Do poems exist as they pretend to
Words scattered on a page they are
Ants pouring out of porous bread
And the search for a meaning among the ants
Is my reward
In the shape of a very personal hallucination

With the precise moment of my pen's scrawling
Down to the very end of this poem
Somewhere, someone, old and sunken will die
Perhaps I should abandon this poem now
Will a better future find him if I were to
I shall then claim to have saved that man
From a far more empathetic life
The dictionary calls death

Our Pawned Hearts

The sequence of objects to become
Lies in a colossal vault of steel wishes
Where dreams are read in pale throats
And the monotony of the future
Is scratched into premonition chips
To ration among the beggars, the men

I won't know until I have finished this stanza
If I will be granted another chance
To write the next
Another honor
To trap the unknown omens of their hearts in words
The enigmas of their minds
And the wagered time of lovers signaling across a lit street in Verona
Or the embrace at the star-crossed plaza in Madrid
The vapor of an afternoon steaming near Jama Masjid
Where the poor romeos hold their first trysts
And scratch out repudiations of a whorish world on walls

Will we ever suffer the errors of chance
That permit us to pen our next stories
Before the exact hour of that sleep
Where if we were to fail it would no longer matter
And nothing will
Even if it is amber colored
And drips down the eyelashes

Long before the origin of the kiss
There was God
And a water color ether of history
A few salamanders
But not a single ounce of pain
Or the corrosion of doubts eating at our Emperors
Like the rust that eats the hangars
There was none of the endless wait dictated by clocks
Or the eyes staring out a restaurant's glass
Certainly no incisions on the stadiums of hearts
Carved by the sprinting icefeet of romeos
It was all a domineering oblivion
For what good is a memory that does not recognize
The starwrecked night of the embraces first
The souls embroiled in centuries old thirst
It was all a world lost to a great lie
A wrong place to be born, the worst world to die

Once upon a time
Nice, cold, usual time
Coursing through life
I got entangled
In an octopus-like solitude
In the lonely evening's barnacles
Until the good memories came oiling me up
And it was easy for me to squeeze through life

Once upon a time
There was a calendar
A cute, colored
Always happy, daily-working calendar
And it would take me from Sunday through Monday
Directly, as if on a bypass
And month after month
For no fault of mine
I kept missing the eighth day of the week
The same eighth day I had promised her stars
And potatoes of that texture perfect
Which make the best smashed potatoes, in her mind
And as it is with fitting jeans and true love
I was never to find

In the crystal sea of my minutes
There is a moment inside all moments
When I peer into the transparency of things
To see light's many shards
There lives a heart
At the end of the neighborhood
That broke into two
Like the beam of that sky lozenge splitting in the branches
When it passed by the shadow of a knife
The dagger of its lover's betrayal
Held in sweaty hands
Constructed of see-through beads

Martha's Wait

Her eyes part a winter lone
Her heart seeks a face familiar
Her throat reckons a rose's groan
And her cheeks regard a tear

Ever still and ever moving
Like the moon that bears a mutiny of million stars
Eyes O lonely Martha's drift
She weaves a corset of sighs and scars

She walks in a hall of conversations
A flower is the expectation in her hair
Let age push you to crisis, let meanings knead your flesh
No man for her here, no man there

Coins ring the hands of men
Disdain your human kind, O men
Far and muted must be their skies
Even with her visible cracks
She eludes them before their craving eyes

When the bells of their churches conquer and toll
Their joints creak up a speech
Their lands and kingdoms come naked and bleak
Like the falsehood of their promises, the emptiness of their reach

Remember, O Martha, the one who waits
In your wait jostle a hundred wait of men
Along with their broken forests washed by winds
And all of their gods, amplifiers and hen

If the shipment of hours
Must bring you burden
And your heart feels a miss
Just wait the insidious night
That sculpts the memory
And the justice of a kiss

The Tectonic Dream

The gigantic slabs of earth
The tectones
Are sliding past the ocean's reflection
Whispering an inimitable lie
As the sliding slabs of our dreams
On the better days
The many seas of feelings
Swirl inside the ivory conchs in our ears
Whispering that this world is the only beautiful world
A world of vast epilogues
Of mammoth whales of sentiments
Of lore, of nightshone shipwrecks
Of sailor shinebodies
Of me
Of you
And our scorching solitude

A few words on the silencing, brutal memories that dawn after the shootings in America.

A Plea For The Choice Of Silence

If your heart, like mine
Seeks a silence tonight
Forbid the one
That succeeds the scarlet note of a bullet
And that follows the grandeur of a gun

Seek not the silence
Of the mothers baptized by tears
Of that drawing room of my America
Where remains now the memory of a child shot dead
Who had once pursued the color of a candy
The little game and the flower red

Seek instead my friend
That urging silence of hope that the morning's sun has shown
And that silencing voice in our stricken souls
That asks how many more God, must we mourn

Solitude Of A Christmas

The surface of water is steel
The shy coonskins
Are out on their heels
From the bough the leaf departs
And the trees stand nude, shivering
Braving the chill and it's showering darts

Passengers and green luggage scents the day
Begetting memories like pups
Somewhere a homebound train sings an old tune
The sun, which is blind and tireless
Comes and sits royally in the eyelashes
A sunray, a vagabond
Highlights the snowflakes in the hair of the laughing girls
Who had once wept for you and for me
In playgrounds open
Pretending it was their hearts that had been broken

These flakes, these leaves
These brooding nocturnal trains
And the nostalgia of homecoming
All meet in secret
In gingerbread house somewhere
And they shall invent yearly, punctual winters
To unleash in Decembers
They shall design the intricate geometry of coldness
That ice-trap the bells and Christmases
The air shall be a shell of egg
Willing to shatter at the arrival of carols

And yet
Even in the forgiving glove of time
On so many days
On so many nights that the moon continues to exalt
My words, my gratitude, my heart
The joys of all poems wait
Searching for the winter apart
Not the winter that an autumn inaugurates
Not the one that benumbs the toes of blue grandmothers
But the winter that hibernates like a glacier's light
In her dream-cheered eyes, hazel and iced
Watching upon the tragic land of man and God
That woman living, unspoken, dear
Who tires never to invade the memories
That woman in a faraway America, meadowed and deep
Where Lincoln, lazy cannons and twilights sleep

Clouds From A Giant's Bread

Clouds are pieces teased from the bread of a giant
On which the child-like angels carve faces and continents
Half-heartedly

A table, like a dictator, is not merely a mind's conjecture
It is the fossil of a prehistoric cow with four legs
The carpenter chopped off its tail and head
To make money, to buy beef for his family's dinner

A museum presents a hollowed cadaver of history and myth
It is in the inside where time has to stop
And ancient mercenaries must freeze in armor suits
Even as their joints ache while a portly tourist looks on

Spiders should not live in cellars
They don't pay rent or gratitude

An old man is finally free of all metaphors of romance
But he is a galley slave of fatigue
And receding, cowardly memories

Birth is the obituary of all things bliss
One who is reading is the one already born
Is the one forever living and tormented

A football stadium is an enormous wreath of tickets and men
And of soda cans, chairs, recurrent curses, nose hair

A horse is the spirit of freedom
And a solidified poem with a tremendous jawline

Our gentleman is really a shaved bear in a suit
History, please shoot him yesterday

She Is El Salvador

She is the daughter of El Salvador
They last saw her sprawled on a hot tar road
After a bullet had split her head and sent her personal eternity
  bleating into oblivion
They photographed her smothered under a tattoo in the shape
  of her man in jeans
She was the prostitute in the booth's cradle crackling in
  a desolate panorama
She was the one with her eye stitched forever by the twines of a
  violent memory
She was a mother with her baby in the air pulsating with the guns

She is the daughter El Salvador
A corset of bandages prettifies her
Rifles serenade her
She had once kissed cocaine colored twilight
Today El Salvador clutches the teats of her own daughters
For the last drops of forgiveness

For those who are sufferers of poems and grief-stricken Septembers.

The Lives Of Others

From here on we live borrowed lives
Once again, my love, lets pass into the great restless sea of otherness
Lets move as the wheat fields and the forests softened by wind
Let us be the serene lake upon which the moon reflects in jewels

We breathe, for someone else must be kept alive
We crawl under the shells of makeups
After the alarm clock burns our sleep forever
We wear the dresses destined for others
Those living in a distant oasis where mirrors map the walls
We open our eyes and we imagine the utopia of others before us
In the basin, in the transparence of glass-air on the streets, in the wallets
We have twins we don't know of
We let the day take us through
And we let the time mark us with a future the other attains
We imagine up Londons
But we wander in the red alleys of Beijing
In the cities with veins frozen out by sun
And the stony clock-towers of Lucknow
Undulating with the many rings of flapping doves
All of this so that we can be that one quicksilver drop
Who has dripped off the edge of sadness
And fallen into love

In between the columns of hours
On a trip in an unknown city
Having had wine, staring past the plaza
Saw standing the two marble cheekbones
Melancholy eyes that passersby wear
Amid raining crystals of sounds
There comes flooding the waters of the dark
There come the colors stabbed by a cone of light
And I turn my eyes
To make them disappear in the air
They lurk like gigantic whales
In guilt's ocean
And I run into them in the hallways strategically placed in the universe
And in the hotel rooms
And in the echo like metal surface in the covert parlors
In all the unimagined worlds

When We Were Young

When we were young
It was Calcutta
We had risen fresh from the smolders
Of the puberty's holocaust
We ruled the decrepit streets
Licking its tar-coated corners
Leaping between ideological gossips
And we combed our hair in unknown mirrors, to win the seams
We fell in love and rose again with knees lacerated
But far more than anything
We tumbled one by one
Into that Saturday of after work hours
Sitting before the phantasmagoria of Facebook
Watching our emaciated memories
And impoverished jaw lines
Searching for that faint, ephemeral trace of happiness
In our own faces

All Chance Is Woman

On the days many and relentless
In the offices that smell of papers and inks
A workingwoman invites the night on her eyelashes
Mascaras and tears are excuse and adventure
And the dressing tables are unrepeatable
But she shall be different every time
In the scald of her daylights elbowing between its panes
Has kohl survived the redemption of rains

On the days many and untold
Poised, blush-cheeked
She passes the side-by-side conference rooms
Did they see her in her peak
When the best afternoons exalted her
Will they kiss her before leaving her to the verdicts of solitude
In the kaleidoscope remote and damp, in her cities wet and cold
Amidst the computers and the rectangles and the forgotten Sundays
A chore queen sits garrisoned by the photon cannons called lamps
Will they testify of her beauty and seduce trepidations in their chests

On the days many on the dates unknown
She hid beneath the blue sunset eyeshadows
Watching over the deleted scenes that is life
Did they respond to her secret subpoenas
Disguised as pleas for help
Or did they choose crack-dens as refuge in her dismissals
Did they propose to her
In the scent of California's sweaty lilacs

On the days many and unseen
She came in high heels
Did they interpret that pony clutter as fate's last knell
Did they walk to her and feel the creases of her botany leaf palm
Did they offer her red wine in cardiac glasses
Will they seek her before the wrinkles do

On nights many and unheard
Away she shall get with the murder at bars
And the screamtrains in her wake
She shall mock the world in hot August
By the tracery of lipsticks
And when they do come drooling
The tumbling men the mumbling men
Crashing one after another
Into the surf of her erstwhile wounds
They will line up as scarlet pimps along graduation halls
Men shall shatter like many sand phantoms
Littered in mercury among the dreamviolins
For
Hell is a famous ambiguity
And all chance is woman

American Serenade

Our ruby Aprils drag us past our homes
To where we have forever known America and her calling
Like the scarred veterans know their brothers
Even before the beginnings of their powdery wars
Sweat-fighting a Kansas mercury sun
Blood red dust trails the last bison
Running past the Texan cemeteries
On America's chest

In our best years determined by rains
We have all sought America in one form or another
Shaved, carved, sabered
By the sinful Oklahoma lightning
Rainrhymers are the birds in her winds
Kissing the dandelions of lovers
Strewn along the dirt back veins of Tennessee
On the boondocks charred by bonfires
Our nostalgia wrapped in barbed wires
Grass scent and speakers

In our immense American solitude
And in our venerable American autumns
Have we all not lived
Wheat and rust
Pickup trucks wading the silver-thick smell of corn
Vast vertebral dust plains and the lone cross
The sweet Alabama dripping skies
That once painted us head to toe in blue
As we walked past the desolate Baptist church
Where on an uncertain altar
In a bleating dusk
A prayer took its last sigh

What Matters Is The Glow

What matters is the glow
That our feet leave in their departing afternoons
Where we came from, the grass tells
Where we shall go, knows the hiding soil
The sky paints naked water
Blue was a famous feeling of birds
My passing away is nothing
Yet another glass of sunlight that shatters in air
Right where the silence had mothered a bouquet of stories
In all the carnival that Nature unleashes
In all its knowing, in all its keeping of our joys
It is sad that I see nothing but into my tiny lens
My own mines, my own possessions, my lifeless private slush
And what shall matter still is the fence
That the hands of our fears shall craft for us

Why Not Merely Her

Why the existence of spastic men on beds?
Why the urging pressures of living the day?
Why feelings?
Why the sparkle of an unexpected tooth in a photograph?
Why her coming at the most vulnerable hour?
Why not two Israels? Why just one?
Why not be granted the meaning of meanings?
Why understand the world when it is empty like an afternoon zoo?
Why time? Why its persistent, haunting slippage?
Why the habit of itch?
Why did Las Vegas drown in dust in the future?
Why trust the bleak skies of Ireland?
Why suffer the ends of springs year after year?
Why the siege of constant winters on widows?
Why they, why us, why we the perishable?
Why do the guavas rot with fragrance?
Why seek the answers, the ones devised long before the questions?
Why breathe for the vanity of a watcher who keeps count?
Why brevity? Why more than a million?
Why flicker in storms?
Why the groan of dying engines on red-hot interstates?
Why remain in memories?
Why clichés outnumbering us?
Why hopes seducing thee?
Why not live a singular, wasteful dream?
Why life?
Why hearts tossed into a stampede of elephants?

Why not merely her, plain and simple?
Why also Adam, why him?
Why her unquestioned justifications?
And why her unheralded whim?

54

Woman Is Any Dusk

Her absence
Is a mother

Of another Nile
Called silence

Her memory
Brings a nonprofit symphony

Of the blind rains
That are set to murder the dust

And uncover the earthworms
Knitting time in the depths

So what if I succumb once more
In my nightly waits of her dusks

Doesn't Greece die
Year after year

My Hour And My Scripture

Every hour lived
Is a hallucination earned
Every Bible preached
Is a scripture burned

To be a bird was her will
Go tear against the gale
Explode in an autumn of feathers, like a story of words
Shower the alleys that the summer dust plasters
And become the keepsakes of lovers of lost hope
Incarcerated in between the pages of Shakespeare
To fly high, to fly high
And witness the forgiveness of a human tear
Crawl down the cheeks
And drip into the mouths going dry
To be a bird was her will
To compel man's soul
Who on an afternoon palpates death's delight

To fly high, to fly high
Watch civilizations froth and abound
From heavens in their blued gold
To persist constant
The inferno of their breasts
Of brides reposed in rest
To watch mothers lonely in cold straw huts
And the breeding of vast rivers in between
Their remote child toiling the provinces of happiness

To be a bird
Is to know not
Is to believe not
That in man's city cruel
One flies high
And by the strict method of running into the building glass pane
Die

An Appeal For Correctness

If in one line of God I were to believe
If in one word of delight I were to grieve
If in one season of seconds I were to live
If in one good heart I were to give
If there be one splendor of rain for inmate each
If each toil of the slave become his master's breach
If there be no more authority of plagues on Africa's nights
If there be a stage of world untouched by fights
If there be one grain perpetual on every tongue
A shard of bliss for the old, a confession for the young
If there be a flower for her clearest tear
If men escape never the certification of fear
Then, Lord, do not hold these glories my moments lack
Return the scar-less skin that once draped her back

Vast meadows have spread open
The horses patterned on them
Suckling nourishment in Kentucky
One day you are on the asphalt
Snaking down the earth's bosom
And the other end is a visit
Long in a slew of cars
Silent and music toned their sliding
The highway is my passage
My growing, my youth, my boredom, my old age

My memory is stretched between two points
The false awareness of my birth
The daze of a death coming
There are days
When memory seems like a mere instant
A plunge of needle in the feeling's flesh
And birth and death seem the same, overlapping truths

The lover knows no forbidden surfaces
Or warnings, or regrets
Or it is what creates a lover in the first place
We go visit our lovers
Our ends, our whisper from an unknown far
Hands reach out they will
Hands I shall not refuse
For all my life
Hands so evasive I shall never touch
In all my journey

A poem for us, we who wake up thirsty in the middle of night and ravage about the house for water – the good, clean, moral, city tap water.

In The Silence Of A Mortal's Bedroom

Popping out from a long human assembly line
We, the mortals, have escaped our wombs
We slide into our personal futures
Some rich some poor, some calm some boor
Pushed about in a soup of city crowd
When the good fate prevails in you
We will see you in schools
When the good fate fails in you
We will see you in ghettos
A coppersmith called poverty dents my face
We will take a few among us for heroes
And we will shoot them in Memphis
A few among us will be zeroes
Drowning in bars
We shall gild your words
We shall tie it to the dove
We shall shred it to pieces
At the altar of love
We shall chase the women
We shall have our eras of vices
And we shall hate it to the core
We shall make plastic celebrities
We shall love them in lore
But our bodiless inventions
Shall always know us more

With twigs in our hands we go round and round
We shall mark our nations on the patient ground
We simmer them an anthem
Only to drag them by their petticoats, hooks in their daughter's scars
Their nations, my nation, now the whore of our wars
We shall scale our Vaticans all cloaked red
We shall be in the stories inscribed on beds
We shall plaster you on hoardings
We shall wreath you in talks
Mortal we shall live
Mortal we shall rather not die
We shall escape forever the noiseless wombs
Only to nurse our dripping wounds
In the silence of our inner bedrooms

The Day After The Oklahoma Tornado

If she comes looking
For one Oklahoma
What words will she bear
For her Oklahoma
She who in a night past
Was the feather in the tornado vast
Hauled by her flanks
Flung dead in a rain of metal
Silent among the needles of planks

To see Oklahoma in so much change
All in one decisive night
No longer she shall see
Her feet-pressed path to the school
No longer the feel of grass
No longer her daddy in smiles
But lint, dead dogs and glass
Spread miles and miles

Not anymore her town memorable and dear
But a poem sad of many a tear
Twilight stitched up in unearthed graves
Only the solitary stars and stripes stood saved
The grief of eyes searching her in albums and stars
Searching beside a twisted congregation of cars

If she comes looking today
For one Oklahoma
In its destruction
She might recall the horrible day
All steel splintered and grey
When the night worn
Was all confetti torn
Where did you go Oklahoma
O you are no longer the same
Do you have a new name
I still have my praises for you
The songs I wrote, soap bubbles I blew
In the first words they taught me in your school
The words in which Your Bible
Printed we still keep
In which once we daily prayed
And in which now we daily weep

A Pact With Solitude

Many years ago, many silences away
I made a pact with solitude
I shall bear your haunting sobriety, said I
I shall grant poetry in return, said solitude

So many good autumns had gone by in the window
So many words came visiting
Golden words about what abides and what lives measureless
But none to adorn the silent whiteness of my pages
It was rather a murmur
A noise unrelenting into which everything dissolved
My seas, the textures of my imagined islands
Everything dissolved and was scattered
Greater and greater, and less than nothing

In that mutiny of images, in that betrayal of letters
I asked solitude mine
How do I ever get these on the page
When the letters refuse to line

These are not meant for the ink, said solitude
You must string them in blood
Look at your shirt, haven't you noticed
Go seek the judgment of a mirror
See that scarlet seeping in your heart my dear
Remember the time once, years ago, when you chose me
And she was not here

ABOUT THE AUTHOR

Nishíth Singh was born in an arid, red-soiled town in the Indian subcontinent before moving to America where he currently resides as a writer.

www.ingramcontent.com/pod-product-compliance
Lightning Source LLC
Chambersburg PA
CBHW020604030426
42337CB00013B/1203